STANISŁAW KLIMEK

WROCŁAW

Architecture and History

text by
Rafał Eysymontt

WYDAWNICTWO VIA NOVA
2001

Photos:	Stanisław Klimek
Text:	Rafał Eysymontt
Translation:	Małgorzata Możdżyńska-Nawotka Andrzej Głazek
Editors:	Wiesław Cwojdziński Agnieszka Gola Elżbieta Klimek Anna Kosmulska Agnieszka Środek

Engraving on page 1 belongs to the collection
of the University Library in Wrocław.
Engraving on page 2 belongs to the collection
of the Museum of Architecture in Wrocław.

Wydawnictwo VIA NOVA
50 077 Wrocław, ul. Kazimierza Wielkiego 39
tel. (+48/71) 44-23-77, fax (+48/71) 44-23-77
www.vianova.com.pl

M. Haulbein, 1668

In 1460, Aeneas Sylvius Piccolomini – who was later to become Pope Pius II – wrote: 'Wrocław is a very big city on the Odra river, with beautifully decorated private and public buildings'. Our predecessors often referred to the Wrocław bishopric as 'golden'. On the other hand, J.W. Goethe wrote in 1790: 'We are again in this noisy, dirty, stinking Wrocław, but I hope to be able to escape from here soon...' These two extreme opinions refer to a city of an ambiguous and fascinating character. At various moments of its history Wrocław was a powerful town, becoming at other times considerably weakened and subordinated to a host of rulers, some of whom were mighty, some less so. Pledged by sovereigns as security for loans, it was on some occasions a mere pawn in the game of dynastic politics. The city's political status changed as well: from the capital of the independent Duchy of Silesia, to a Bohemian and even Hungarian city (a brief episode from 1479 to 1490); subsequently ruled by the Jagiellonian dynasty until 1526, it remained under the imperial House of Habsburg for the next 215 years. Throughout the entire period, Wrocław demonstrated considerable reserve and constraint in its political engagement, which for centuries enabled the city to protect its independence and foster economic prosperity. After short periods of temporary decline, Wrocław was taken over by the young Prussian state in 1757 and between 1849 and 1914 it became a truly modern city, its population growing from 100,000 to 540,000.

Every period in the city's history has left its architectural heritage, shaped by religious and political doctrines, long-lasting trends and passing fashions, as well as real and imagined needs of its population. This richness and diversity contribute to the city's specific *genius loci*, bred throughout history on its consciously cosmopolitan ambitions combined with an attachment to this particular place in the marshy and vast valley of the Odra River. As the Silesian historian Martinus Zeller so simply expressed it in 1640: 'Wrocław is located in a beautiful, flat terrain'.

The only sources of information about prehistoric Wrocław prior to A.D. 1000 are the recovered fragments of objects left behind by the people who lived there from the Bronze Age through the period of Slavonic tribal states. Of these, closest to Wrocław were the lands of the *Slezanie* that stretched around the sacred mountain of Ślęża located about 30 kilometres south-west of today's Wrocław. The existence of this population and the presence of an organized society was possibly the reason for the diplomatic efforts undertaken by Boleslaus the Brave – who was later to become Poland's first king – to have a bishopric established here, which was accomplished in the year 1000. On that occasion, the name 'Wrotizlava' appeared for the first time, mentioned by the German chronicler Thietmar. The conversion of Silesia to Christianity and the establishment of several new bishoprics in Poland, including the one in Wrocław, followed the martyrdom and subsequent canonisation of St. Adalbert, the bishop of Prague, who was killed by the heathen Prussians during his evangelising mission in

Pomerania. He was canonised by Pope Sylvester I, largely due to the efforts of King Boleslaus. These developments tied Wrocław to the Polish state then ruled by the Piast dynasty. Located close to Bohemia, where the Slavonic martyr saint had come from, and to the residences of Otto III in Saxony, where the Holy Roman Empire was being restored, Wrocław was from the beginning the centre of the south-western part of the Piast state. Following the death of Bolesłaus III Wrymouth in 1138 and the subsequent division of Poland into five duchies, Wrocław became the capital of the Duchy of Silesia and later of all of Lower Silesia, which it has remained ever since despite frequent changes, first in terms of the feudal system of fiefdoms and then of the city's national status.

The first cluster of dwellings in the area of the present-day Wrocław was a regularly laid out settlement fortified by a rampart of log construction characteristic of Slavonic tribal villages. It was situated on an island on the Odra, which provided good natural defence against any attacks. Within a stretch of a dozen or so kilometres from the island, four tributaries (the Oława, Widawa, Ślęza, and Bystrzyca rivers) flow into the Odra. The island, which has retained its historical name of Ostrów Tumski (Cathedral Island), is now only partially surrounded by water. Following this first settlement, new villages soon emerged as competitive trade centres. They were located at several sites: on the island itself, by the market place adjacent to the castle; at the site where St. Adalbert's Church was later built; by the present St. Maurice's Church, where the *platea Romana* settlement of Walloon weavers was confirmed in documents as early as the 12th century; and possibly also at three other sites west of the present-day city centre: Sokolniki, Szczepin, and Nabytyn. The most important of them was the **trade settlement by St. Adalbert's Church** (the church was founded in 1112), situated about 1.2 km south-west of Ostrów Tumski. The Slavonic martyr Adalbert had fulfilled an apostolic mission and become the patron saint of the emerging urban civilisation, which was built around the trade exchange flourishing at the crossroads of two major trade routes: the North-South 'amber' route and the East-West route leading from Kievan Rus. Emerging at the crossroads, the new centre proved the vitality of the community which 150 years later would build a new town, this time on a geometrical layout, halfway between the original tribal settlement on Ostrów Tumski and the old market place by St. Adalbert's Church. Around 1000, a stone cathedral was erected on Ostrów Tumski, several hundred meters east of the old stronghold, as an expression of the connection between the temporal power of the Piast rulers and the religious foundation of their state. These three centres – the castle, the market place, and the cathedral –became three magnets attracting a population of craftsmen and merchants, who were the core of any urban community.

Our knowledge of the first structures erected in Wrocław comes solely from archaeological findings. The dwellings were fairly typical cabins built of oak and pine logs. The entire settlement was fortified by ramparts of timber compartments filled with earth and stones, which divided the whole into three basic units: an inner yard with a somewhat more prominent residential hall; an outer bailey with farm buildings; and a colony of houses built around the cathedral. The cathedral was the city's first stone structure. Little is known of its architectural form. The second cathedral was erected on the same site when the bishop of Wrocław was one Walter of Malonne, who had arrived in the city in 1158 from the diocese of Liege on the Meuse, in today's Belgium. The new cathedral was a typical monumental Romanesque structure, terminating in a semicircular apse on the east side, with a western façade emphasized by two towers which symbolized the connection between the authority of the Church and the power of the ruling dukes. The builders of the cathedral drew inspiration from churches of Northern Italy, which at that time were the most advanced form of ecclesiastical architecture. The form of Italian churches was based on Early Christian basilicas, which had always remained the supreme ideal of the Princes of the Church and founders of monastic orders – the restorers of European civilisation. In this way, Wrocław came for the first time under the direct influence of the Mediterranean culture radiating from centres more distant than Prague or Saxony. This influence would repeatedly prove vital in the city's later architectural history, reappearing in many Renaissance, Baroque, and Neoclassical buildings.

Following the cathedral, the first **convents and monasteries** were soon founded in the city. The oldest extant records of the Benedictine Abbey of St. Martin, located on Wyspa Piaskowa (Sand Island), date back to 1149. Its chapel was later to become St. Martin's chapel of the ducal castle. One of the most influential abbeys of Mediaeval Poland was the Benedictine Abbey founded at the nearby Ołbin by the magnate Piotr Włost. The complex comprised the monumental St. Vincent's basilica, whose architectural form was inspired by Early Christian predecessors, and the church of St. Michael. Such was the splendour of the Ołbin abbey that when it was demolished in 1529, the townspeople decided to save some of the sculptures, which were subsequently built into the walls of other churches, including St. Mary Magdalene's. Like the remnants of the Romanesque cathedral, the sculptures from Ołbin were executed in the best North Italian style. In the 12th century, the Augustinian friars summoned from Arrovaise had their abbey erected on Wyspa Piaskowa, on the site of the existing Church of the Blessed Virgin Mary. Probably not as monumental as the Ołbin complex, the Augustinian monastery comprised a church, which is represented on a tympanum commemorating its foundation, still to be seen in the temple later built on the same site. Like the cathedral, the church had two towers in the western façade.

The tradition of erecting new sanctuaries on the site of older churches, so important in the Middle Ages, makes it possible for us today to grasp the scale of 12th-century Wrocław. With a stretch of about two kilometres between the city's two outermost sites – the Ołbin Abbey located on the Odra's right bank and the left-bank St. Adalbert's Church – Wrocław was one of the biggest towns in this part of Europe. The 12th-century city comprised the monumental stone structures discussed earlier, the connecting roads, several wooden bridges across the Odra, the ducal residence situated west of the cathedral and colonies of wooden houses, which were built mostly along roads and at crossroads. People were coming to the city even from distant areas seeking protection from robbers, not to mention the new urban lifestyle and the prospect of eternal life, attainable only through participation in the Holy Mass celebrated in the city's monumental churches. The ducal presence in the local residence gave Wrocław the most prominent position among Silesian urban centres compared not only to the towns founded nearby in the early 13th century (Trzebnica, Środa Śląska, Niemcza) but also to those situated further away (for example Legnica, which in the early 13th century already had two churches and a castle).

Henry the Bearded, who ruled from 1201 as the first of several distinguished Silesian dukes, had reasons for choosing Wrocław as his ducal residence. With its central location on the river banks and at the crossroads of important trade routes, and with its busy market place already established, Wrocław could generate a much higher income for the duke than any other town in Silesia to finance the construction of an imposing castle. However, the duke had underestimated the competition from the rapidly growing town itself and from the Wrocław bishopric. The construction of the castle on Ostrów Tumski was never finished. Also, the castle's 'modern octagonal chapel, with its architectural references to the symbolic meanings of the circle and the square, of earth and heaven – a sign of unity between temporal power and divine authority' was left uncompleted. God's favour seemed to rest more on the bishop than on the duke as ecclesiastical structures grew in number and magnificence, while no ducal palace of any grandeur was ever completed. The conflict between the Wrocław bishops and dukes had a symbolic outcome. The clash of Henry the Bearded's grandson Duke Henry Probus and Bishop Thomas was resolved in a covenant between the two, and Henry erected the most magnificent Gothic church in Wrocław – the collegiate Church of the Holy Cross. Soon, the ducal residence was moved from Ostrów Tumski to the Odra's left bank, to the site presently occupied by the Baroque complex of the University. However, there is no trace of the castle itself in the present-day layout of the city.

Also on the Odra's left bank a rectangular market place – today's **Nowy Targ (New Market)** – was established by Henry the Bearded as the first step in a new phase of colonization activity linked probably to the Magdeburg Law (*Ius Teutonicum*), which was adopted for Wrocław in 1211. Nearby, along the first streets laid out by means of a boning-rod, residential buildings were erected, including the so called *curia* (urban residence) of the abbesses of the Trzebnica convent, mentioned as early as 1208. Soon, many craftsmen would settle in the vicinity, probably moving here from several nearby villages, including Kowale, Sokolniki, Świątniki, or Żyrdniki (later Żerniki) – settlements of serf craftsmen forced to labour for the Wrocław dukes. Their trades gave names to the newly laid-out streets. Thus, the process of the urban development was initiated, in time leading to the emergence of a town – a free conglomerate of many families pursuing various trades and selling their products on the free market. However, these newly acquired urban liberties also benefitted the Wrocław dukes as they contributed to the increase of their income. Three roads connecting the new town to Kraków, two roads leading to Toruń and Gdańsk, one to Saxony, and two to Bohemia and Moravia made it easy and profitable for merchants to set up their warehouses and stalls in the town, along with inns and lodgings. During this period, several new churches were built for the townspeople, such as **St. Mary Magdalene's**, erected in 1226, to which services were transferred from St. Adalbert's Church when the latter was given to the newly-arrived Dominican friars. Also, the first **St. Elizabeth's Church** was erected in the early 13th century. The original structure of that church, in which an Early Gothic vaulting was combined with the predominantly Romanesque architecture characteristic of churches built by the mendicant preaching orders in the mid-13th century, was later replaced by the extant imposing Gothic temple. **St. Maurice's Church** and **St. Nicholas' Church** were also built in the early 13th century.

The area stretching between the city's two principal and largest churches – St. Elizabeth's and St. Mary Magdalene's – was the scene of the central event in the development of Wrocław. In 1241, soon after the wooden houses on the Odra's left bank were destroyed during the Tartar invasion, Wrocław was endowed with city statutes in accordance with the Magdeburg Law. Following this first grant of city rights, the city's locator (in the Middle Ages an organizer and surveyor of a newly-founded settlement) laid out an imposing rectangular **town square** called the **Rynek** and a rectangular grid of streets connected to Nowy Targ, which had been founded several dozen years earlier. These developments were crucial as they meant not only a fundamental change in Wrocław's legal status, but also a transition from a fortified settlement established on an oval plan (similar to the colony on Ostrów Tumski) to a rectangular arrangement characterized by straight lines and right angles. It was a transition from the 'natural' form, more or less accidental and determined primarily by characteristics of the terrain, to the form intentionally imbued with abstract and aesthetic qualities. As a result of this urban planning process, Wrocław was completely reshaped from a colony of houses grouped quite chaotically along roads and around crossroads into a city built on a purposefully arranged geometric gridiron pattern. Once chosen, this underlying structure has ever since remained an indispensable component of the city. The centre of the new town – the newly laid-out Rynek and the adjacent Plac Solny (Salt Market)– took over the marketplace functions from the original location by St. Adalbert's Church. Here in the Rynek, the first merchant house was built for travelling merchants, to be later replaced by the Town Hall erected on the same site. As the Tartar invasion showed, the prosperous urban centre required better protection against potential attacks. Around the mid-13th century, the construction of city walls with seven gates began. In order to provide a new momentum for the city's further development, Duke Henry III endowed Wrocław, at that time already completely surrounded by fortified walls, with new city charters in 1261. In 1263 the Duke also founded the so called **New Town** to the east of St. Adalbert's Church; it remained an independent entity only until 1327.

The two Romanesque parish churches mentioned above, **St. Mary Magdalene's** and **St. Elizabeth's**, and also the small **St. Egidius' Church** by the Cathedral, were built of brick, which around that time was beginning to replace stone in newly erected monumental structures. However, the leading role in the transfer of the latest European architectural trends was played by the Wrocław bishopric and monasteries. Taken over by the friars, **St. Adalbert's Dominican Church** underwent remodelling: the new temple was also built of brick but the structure and proportions were totally different. During the same period, a new **Franciscan Church** was erected in today's Nankiera Square and **the Cathedral's new chancel** showed the influence of French Cistercian architecture. These three churches testify to the leading role played by the new monastic orders in the formation of the local architectural style. The monumental brick architecture of churches erected by monastic orders, with its stress on clearly defined architectural shapes and the functional quality of spacious interiors rather than on decorative stone detail, remained the basic mode of ecclesiastical architecture in Wrocław throughout the 14th century.

The third quarter of the 13th century was marked by the beginning of several major construction projects which were continued through the end of the 15th century. In 1420, there were already 37 churches in Wrocław. Due to their individual character and originality as well as certain unique architectural qualities, the buildings erected during that period have remained the most specific element of the city's architectural landscape. If one takes into consideration that two hundred years separate the construction of the choir of the Franciscan Church, which was erected in 1270, from the completion of the western sections of the **Corpus Christi Church** or the Bernardine Church, their stylistic uniformity is amazing. It is remarkable that when the new western section of St. Adalbert's Dominican Church was erected after 1492, the builders referred directly to the architectural proportions of its extant chancel completed some 200 years earlier, around 1300. No matter how diverse were the founders or benefactors of these edifices and the relevant artistic influences deciphered by art historians, or how different the structural and spatial organization of the churches – which included basilicas, hall churches, and even a two-storey church – the basic elements of style remained constant. There was definitely a certain spirit common to Wrocław's Gothic architecture, permeating all these buildings except for two smaller churches: **St. Barbara's** and **St. Christopher's**. The people of Wrocław frequently analyse the spirit pervading the city's architecture, trying to pin down its components and wondering whether certain features characteristic of the Wrocław Gothic could have been passed on to the city's Baroque buildings or even its modern architecture. Is there not a certain general compact and monumental quality about the buildings erected in Wrocław during different historical periods along with an affinity for imposing, massive towers (and later for imposing, massive cupolas) combined with façades characterized by distinctively repetitive rhythms? The elongated and rhythmically divided façades of such buildings as – for example – the **Church of the Blessed Virgin Mary** on Wyspa Piaskowa on the one hand and the Baroque **University** on the other, reflect the plain countryside of the Odra lowlands, while the lack of any natural vertical accents is compensated for by monumental towers dominating the landscape. The extant spires of the Cathedral, St. Mary Magdalene's, or St. Elizabeth's (the tallest of all Wrocław towers) are there for all to see but there were also some never-completed projects, such as the University tower or the skyscrapers designed by Max Berg in the 1920s, particularly the one intended for the site between the city's two principal bridges: today's Pokoju Bridge and Grunwaldzki Bridge.

The most characteristic of these buildings are the two **parish churches – St. Mary Magdalene's** and **St. Elizabeth's** – which replaced the original Romanesque structures discussed earlier following the great fire of 1342. Like all monumental Gothic edifices, they were erected in stages by large organizations of builders established in order to carry out such projects. The construction work on St. Mary Magdalene's started from the church's western sections and the choir was not completed until after 1470. The builders of St. Elizabeth's began from the choir, so the westernmost bay of the vault was finished as late as the mid-15th century. Despite the long construction periods, both churches are imposing elongated structures of striking unity: the effect is reinforced by the lack of any transept (transverse arms of a cross-shaped church, usually between nave and chancel). In this respect, both parish churches followed the local tradition originating in the Cathedral, where an extended severy was used for the first time instead of a transept to separate the choir (reserved for the clergy and patriciate) from the nave, which was accessible to the faithful of a lesser social standing. An even higher degree of spatial unity was achieved in the **Church of the Blessed Virgin Mary**, where the length of the tunnel-like nave is not interrupted even by a widened bay of a vault. The sanctuary was built as a hall-church with magnificent stellar and tripartite vaults. Especially remarkable was the intention to serve an expanding community of townspeople in this cloister church, apparent in the selection of the hall system, which conveyed an impression of architectural unity and was conducive to the participation of all the faithful in liturgy performed in an integrated and imposing house of worship. In 1351, in the street leading to the Świdnica Gate on the opposite side of the town, Emperor Charles IV, the King of Bohemia, founded **St. Dorothy's Church** for the Augustinian friars. St. Dorothy later became the patron saint of the Town Hall chapel and of the entire city. First, an elongated choir was erected. As was typical of cloister churches, St. Dorothy's had a main choir only, with no side choirs. Built by a Bohemian master builder of the famous Parler family, the structure nevertheless retained all the basic elements of the unique style associated with the Wrocław Gothic. Some twenty years later, the body of the church was completed as a hall interior with a nave and two aisles of equal height.

The collegiate **Church of the Holy Cross** – a unique structure dominating the city's architectural landscape – was founded in 1288 by Henry IV Probus, the most distinguished of the Silesian dukes and the most powerful contender for the Polish throne. In 1290, Henry himself was buried here. This magnificent architectural monument, located several hundred meters west of the Cathedral, is one of Wrocław's two Gothic churches distinguished by a pronounced transept. Moreover, the church is a two-storey structure. This arrangement probably resulted from the fact that when the western section was built, some fifty years after the completion of the chancel, its floor level had to conform to the extant floor of the eastern part, which was elevated because of a high crypt located underneath, designated as a burial place for members of the ducal family. The exterior architecture of the church is very solid, but at the same time enlivened by an intense sculptural quality lent by the many buttresses and a tower with an original pointed Gothic spire. It is worth mentioning that the famous astronomer Nicholas Copernicus was a canon of the collegiate Church of the Holy Cross. Among the church's attractions, there is also an original 14th-century Silesian eagle of imposing size, made of copper, on the southern façade.

In any case, the Gothic architecture in Wrocław testifies to the impressive power of the city's burghers. In addition to serving religious purposes, church buildings performed important public functions for the urban community. Not unlike the Greek *agora*, any prominent Mediaeval church was a meeting place suitable for social contacts, communication exchange, and a display of wealth. During the 15th century, chapels built adjacent to the two principal parish churches – St. Mary Magdalene's and St. Elizabeth's – became a form of such display, financed by prominent burghers or by entire trade guilds. During the period marked by the splendid development of ecclesiastical architecture in Wrocław around the mid-14th century, the first local builders' workshops were founded. The name of one Master Peschke repeatedly appears in documents referring to several construction projects, including the main part of the Cathedral's nave, St. Mary Magdalene's and the Church of the Blessed Virgin Mary. The style of the above mentioned churches is frequently referred to as 'reductive Gothic' and is characterized as possessing some archaic features reflective of a certain traditionalism expressed through direct references to the already outmoded Romanesque architecture of cloister churches. The burghers of Wrocław, who undoubtedly had their say in decisions pertaining to the architectural shape of the churches, probably wanted them to be like the sanctuaries erected by their ancestors and deliberately perpetuated the tradition of those venerable places of worship, which in previous centuries had been provided to the townsfolk by religious orders. This kind of respect for tradition was alive even a century later, as exemplified by the western portico entrance to the Cathedral, whose construction began in 1465. For this ornate structure, the master builders Hans Berthold and Peter Franczke used forms imitating classical Romanesque architecture to accentuate the church's ancient origin. The same team of artists demonstrated a similar attitude while remodelling the gable of the Mayor's Hall in the southern façade of the Town Hall during the period of 1450–1470.

The most imposing monument testifying to the power of Wrocław burghers is the **Town Hall**. The building's origins date back to 1299, when the first structure was erected on this site, next to the merchant house situated in the middle of the Rynek. The Town Hall's present form was eventually defined at the turn of the 15th and 16th centuries after some two hundred years of continuous remodelling and expansion, which reflected the growing prestige of the city. The participation of many artists in the subsequent stages of the building activity did not detract from the consistency and harmony of their work's final result. Unlike the parish churches, decorated with a certain deliberate restraint, the Town Hall was lavishly endowed with architectural detail expressing the city's wealth and pride. We can still see this in the 'palatial' oriel of St. Dorothy's chapel, where a reliquary of the city's patron saint was kept; in the portals adorned with crests and heraldic beasts of monarchs ruling at the time (the lion of the Bohemian House of Luxemburg in the outer eastern portal, dated 1360, and the raven of Matthias Corvinus, the King of Hungary, in one of the inner portals executed about a hundred years later); in the southern façade with its 'defensive' castle-like turrets and grotesque reliefs showing the townsfolk imitating knightly games. Trumpets played at noon and in the evening from a tall tower, adjoining the building on the north-west, defining the rhythm of life. Like the ducal castle at an earlier time, the Town Hall presented a hierarchical arrangement of chambers and halls. In the cellar, beer and wine were served. The ground floor was designated for entertainment of the entire town community. The Great Hall on the first floor, with sculptures of knights adorning its walls and ceiling and portals decorated with royal crests, provided a fitting ambience for tournaments organized by members of the patriciate who tried to emulate knights.

At the peak of the development of the city in its Gothic form around the mid-14th century, there were many brick buildings in Wrocław in addition to the churches, the city walls, and the Town Hall. To some extent, this was the result of a regulation ordering new houses to be built of brick issued by the city council in 1363 following a series of devastating fires. Today, some of these stately **Gothic townhouses** still remain hidden under Renaissance or Baroque façades. In the 19th century, many were converted to tenement houses. Today, their bygone glory can be glimpsed only in basements and on ground floors, where the original vaulted ceilings have occasionally survived; in some backyard walls with late Gothic gables and architectural detail still visible (most of the extant examples can be seen on the western side of the Rynek); and in fragments of architectural detail exhibited in the Museum of Architecture. Undoubtedly, **urban residences** called *curiae* were even more grand. Among them were the palaces belonging to the dukes of Lubusz, Opole or Brzeg, located in the vicinity of today's Szewska, Kuźnicza, and Wita Stwosza Streets. The only completely preserved residential building with some Mediaeval architectural features – although combined with certain Early Renaissance elements – is the Cathedral Chapter House situated north-east of the Cathedral.

In addition to residential houses and palaces, commercial buildings were also erected in the city. The character and number of such facilities reflected the number of craftsmen active in Wrocław: in 1473, there were 1197 registered guild masters representing 100 different trades. The layout of the old **Cloth Hall**, which was located north of the Town Hall, remains apparent in the arrangement of narrow houses along the two lanes in the central block of the Rynek. In Malarska Street, the original **butchers' stalls** survive. The **granary** in today's Cieszyńskiego Street, built in 1459 and later converted into an **Arsenal**, remains one of only a few extant Mediaeval structures of this kind in the world (today it houses a branch of the Historical Museum). Like all other developed urban entities, Wrocław also had other public facilities used by the townspeople with greater or lesser frequency, including the still extant prison in Więzienna Street and a whipping-post located east of the Town Hall (now replaced by a replica), along with numerous **hospitals, schools** and the so-called **houses of good maidens**.

Despite its easily defended location at the confluence of the Odra and Oława rivers, Wrocław could not depend on natural water barriers alone for its safety. A **system of triple city walls** was erected, as shown on a magnificent 1562 panorama of the city. The fortifications were built in stages: the construction of the second ring of city walls started around the mid-14th century, and work on the third ring began in the second half of the 15th century. It was a complex system, with many towers (50 in 1512) and gates. Of these gates, the most important were the Oława Gate on the eastern side, the Świdnica Gate on the south, and the St. Nicholas Gate on the west side. Fitted with barbicans (elliptical outworks defending the entrance) and after 1479 with bastilles (defensive structures projecting outwards), the gates were miniature fortresses in their own right. Altogether, in 1512 Wrocław had seven gates and nine wickets. By opening and closing these gates during the day, the traffic of visitors arriving in the city was controlled depending on which of the city's inner streets were more or less jammed. In addition to their defensive function, the gates also provided an opportunity to display the power of the city and its patriciate. Like the Town Hall and castles of feudal lords, they were appointed with chapels and decorated with religious symbols particularly relevant during the period when the Catholic faith seemed threatened, first by the Hussite heresy during the first half of the 15th century and then by the Turkish invasion in the early 16th century. The sculptural decoration of the St. Nicholas Gate was exceptionally magnificent. It included a monumental Crucifix, now built into the façade of the 19th-century Church of Eleven Thousand Virgins in today's Jedności Narodowej Street.

❧

The Renaissance did not leave an impression as profound as the previous period on Wrocław art. After 1526, when the city came under the rule of the House of Habsburg, Wrocław did not participate in the founding of new churches to the same extent as previously. Throughout the rest of the 16th century and in the 17th century, the city was immersed in the religious conflicts so characteristic of the epoch. In the 16th century, however, the principal parish churches were for some time shared by Catholics and Protestants, which testifies to a certain level of mutual tolerance. Any construction work at church buildings was carried out only in case of some sudden necessity. Such a situation occurred when the gigantic **spire crowning the tower of St. Elizabeth's Church** was blown off in 1529. The event was pronounced a miracle as the falling chunk did not kill or injure anyone. The new Renaissance spire has ever since remained the dominant vertical accent in the city's architectural landscape. Another Renaissance spire, the work of Andreas Stellauf of Świdnica, was placed on the tower of the Town Hall. Renaissance spires were also executed for St. Mary Magdalene (1564–1581) and the Cathedral (1556–1586) but have not survived.

The typical Renaissance personage was an individual patron of the arts. Whether a man of cloth or a burgher, his activity was frequently focused on erecting his own monument which resulted in many splendid **tombs and epitaph plaques**, oftentimes executed during the founder's lifetime. In the tombstone of Peter Jenckwitz in **St. Elizabeth's Church**, the harbingers of the Renaissance style appeared – according to some authors as the first manifestation of the new mode of expression north of the Alps – as early as the late 15th and early 16th century. Not surprisingly, many such monuments can be found in the two principal churches serving the city's burghers, St. Mary Magdalene's and St. Elizabeth's. The tomb of Bishop Turzon, the most distinguished among the Wrocław humanists of the first half of the 16th century, can still be admired in the Cathedral. Patrons with humanist ambitions frequently built new residences with fashionable gardens, like the garden of the famous Wrocław botanist **Laurentius Scholz**, which used to be situated in today's Wierzbowa Street but has not survived.

During the 16th century, the ducal castle on the Odra's left bank ceased to play any significant role and the emperor, who visited Wrocław on several occasions, received homage in the **House of the Seven Electors** located on the western side of the Rynek. Another splendid **patrician palatial house** was the residence of the humanist Heinrich Rybish in today's Ofiar Oświęcimskich Street. Of this Renaissance complex, erected in 1526–1531, only a fragment has survived, including the main portal with a unique scene depicting a woman in labour. Famous at the time for its magnificent Renaissance parapet, the grand **Golden Crown House**, which used to stand on the corner of the Rynek and Oławska Street, is known today only from old photographs. As in the 16th century the radiant Rynek was already surrounded by imposing gabled Gothic townhouses, and it was difficult to find plots wide enough to accommodate new fashionable residences of the Italian urban *palazzo* type with their characteristic long, horizontal façades. With this factor limiting building activity, construction focused instead on the remodelling of existing townhouses' narrow gabled façades in the Renaissance style, which was frequently performed by the best masters brought from the Netherlands. Erected in 1587–1597 by the city architect Friedrich Gross and sculptor Gerhard Hendrik, the **Griffons House** at 2 Rynek, with apocalyptic beasts adorning its gable, remains a magnificent example of the Dutch Renaissance style. The city's economic development during the 16th century also touched some of its commercial buildings which were similarly remodelled, like the butchers' stalls in Jatki Street, where some 16th century *sgraffiti* (plaster decorations consisting of geometrical patterns) have survived. During the same period a building housing the **municipal scales** was erected. The **Cloth Hall**, built west of the Town Hall in 1521, was unfortunately completely altered in the 19th century.

In the 16th century, with fortifications getting more complex as a result of the introduction of firearms, an architect-engineer familiar with all the modern developments became the person most sought-after by the city council as a specialist essential for the city's safety. However, the activity of those artists was not limited to defensive structures, but extended to other buildings which also reflected their familiarity with current architectural trends. The first city architect was one Benedict of Kraków, brought to Wrocław in 1518. As early as the first half of the 16th century, Italian architects became responsible for fortifications in Wrocław. The first of them was Vicenzia da Parmantario, who obtained burgher's rights in 1518. Later this task was carried out by the Italian architect Jakob Paar and Bernard Niuron, of French descent – the team famous for the remodelling of the splendid palace of the Piast dukes in Brzeg. In the late 16th century, the city architect Friedrich Gross, himself a Dutchman, brought over a fortifier Hans Schneider von Lindau from Gdańsk. In the 1630s, Walentin Saebish, the most renowned of Silesian fortification specialists and the first engineer of the period to carry out projects throughout Europe, was also active in Wrocław. Such diversity among city architects in terms of their place of origin mirrored changes occurring with regard to the passing aesthetic trends, which was in turn reflective of the more general shifting of artistic orientation: from Northern Italian art, which had dominated the scene in the first half of the 16th century, to the Dutch influence gaining ground through intense commercial contacts with the Netherlands, associated with the busy trade route leading through Wrocław from Northern Europe to Kievan Rus. Many artists were brought from the Netherlands, while the alabaster used in many of their works came from the vicinity of Lviv in today's Ukraine. Works of famous artists were for the first time imported to Wrocław, including paintings from the workshops of Albrecht Dürer and Lucas Cranach acquired by Bishop Jan Turzon. The exchange of aesthetic ideas and talents between Wrocław and other centres was mutual, as several artist from Wrocław became active at the royal court in Kraków. Two of them – Bartłomiej Strobel and Marcin Köber – attained the position of court painters to Polish kings.

Whereas the most outstanding civilisation and aesthetic achievement of the Gothic period in Wrocław were the city's monumental churches, sculpture became the dominant form of expression in the subsequent periods of Renaissance and Mannerism. There were many **tombstones** built into the walls of parish churches; monumental **tombs** in the Cathedral and other temples; richly decorated **pulpits**, including a magnificent one by Friedrich Gross in St. Mary Magdalene's; and also **baptismal fonts**, like the font in St. Mary Magdalene's. It is impossible to enumerate here all of the outstanding Renaissance and Mannerist works but one cannot miss them during even a short visit to Wrocław's churches.

❦

Although the 17th century, with its first half dominated by the devastating Thirty Years' War of 1618–1648, was not as disastrous for Wrocław as for other Silesian towns, no significant architectural projects were initiated in the city until the third quarter of the century. As a part of the Habsburg domain, Wrocław was ruled in an increasingly authoritarian manner and was made ever more Catholic by means of administrative decrees. Part of this Counter-Reformation movement was the deployment of new Catholic religious orders in the city, beginning with the **Jesuits**, who established their first school in 1638 and took over the old ducal castle in 1658. Soon, the new **convents of the Capuchins, Premonstratensians, Augustinians, Clarists, Knights of St. John (Knights of Malta), and the Order of St. John of God (*boni fratres*)** were founded, which gave rise to a new phase of building activity, the most intense since the Gothic period. Previously predominantly Gothic, the architectural landscape of the city became enriched with many Baroque buildings. However, throughout these developments, the character of Wrocław architecture somehow remained unchanged in its aesthetic expression. The Baroque style – usually so dynamic and autonomous with regard to spatial arrangement and simultaneously combining literary content with painterly qualities – here became the 'Wrocław Baroque': a monumental and 'serious' style adjusted to the specific mode of the local architecture. We can observe this phenomenon in **St. Vincent's Monastery** located opposite the Covered Market: with the façades divided by the repetitive rhythm of vertical pilasters, it remains in perfect harmony with the adjacent Gothic church, framed by rhythmically arranged vertical buttresses. Likewise, the interiors of the town's two biggest Baroque churches (the Church of the Blessed Name of Jesus and St. Anthony's) are divided into bays in the manner so characteristic of Gothic churches. Combined with rows of side chapels, this arrangement creates the effect of a traditional church interior with a nave and two aisles. The basic characteristics of Baroque architecture in Wrocław include the 'Gothic' verticalism and a certain 'additive' quality. Another indispensable element is the contrast, so typical of many prominent Baroque structures in Wrocław, between the buildings' long bodies – composed of vertical elements of essentially Gothic structure, combined in a characteristic 'additive' manner and separated from one another – and their tall towers. Such contrast is exemplified by today's **Ursuline Convent**. Similarly, the original design for the University building included a massive tower balancing the horizontal pull of the elongated structure. The stress on verticality is also evident in the gables of Baroque townhouses framed by slim pilasters or in the gables framing the magnificent riverside façade of the **convent of the Red Star Knights of the Cross (*stelliferi hospitalarii*)** in today's Grodzka Street. Typically a prominent element of Baroque architecture, here the cupola is only one of the components in a composition dominated by triangular gables.

Of course, one cannot say that the architecture of the second half of the 17th century and the first half of the 18th century in Wrocław was completely uniform. There was a dynamic line of development following current artistic tendencies, albeit to a limited degree: initially Wrocław looked up to Italy and later – starting in the late 17th century – to the two principal centres of the Habsburg Empire, Prague and Vienna. Outstanding and creative artists of European renown worked in Wrocław, including the leading Austrian architect Lucas von Hildebrandt, the Frenchman Jean Baptist Mathieu (who designed the convent of the Red Star Knights of the Cross), and Christoph Hackner (designer of the non-extant original **Hatzfeld Palace**). Hackner, known also for the non-extant residence of Lubiąż abbots in Legnica, worked in the best Viennese style, close to the manner of Lucas von Hildebrandt, who designed the **Schreyvogel Palace**, another splendid residence, which unfortunately has not survived. Symbolically, the dates of Hackner's birth and death, 1663–1741, mark the possible turning points in the development of the Baroque architecture in Wrocław.

In addition to 'importing' renowned architects who worked in Wrocław for extended periods, some patrons, particularly Wrocław bishops, imported architectural designs for their projects. Cardinal Frederick of Hesse commissioned the Italian Giacomo Scianzi to design **St. Elisabeth's Chapel** built south of the Cathedral's chancel in 1680–1700. The cardinal's bust by Gianlorenzo Bernini remains situated above the entrance to the chapel. Ludwig von Neuburg, Frederick's successor on the bishop's seat, chose the Viennese architect Johann Fisher von Erlach, one of the period's most successful artists, to design the Elector's Chapel built in 1716–1724 on the other side of the chancel, opposite St. Elizabeth's Chapel. Both chapels are miniature versions of the ideal Baroque interior, with deliberately created unique spatial illusions. Complementing the architecture, sculptures and paintings proclaim the glory of God and their bishop sponsors, God's not so very modest governors in Silesia. Two other Baroque chapels built on a central plan and furnished with equally splendid décor – **Blessed Czesław's Chapel** adjacent to the Dominican St. Adalbert's Church and **Hochberg's Chapel** of St. Vincent's Church, founded by Count Hochberg and designed by Christoph Hackner – were created by local artists.

A mong the prominent architects of the 18th-century Wrocław, one has to mention the Jesuit Christoph Tausch, who worked on the interior design of the city's largest Baroque complex: the Jesuit college and church, later to be converted into a university. Erected in 1728–1744, the **University**, to which all of the outstanding local 18th-century architects contributed (Hackner, Tausch, Peitner), represents the final stage in the development of Baroque architecture in Wrocław, although the project was never fully completed. The building combines certain features typical of Wrocław architecture with forms developed in other Jesuit colleges in Silesia (Legnica, Nysa, Głogów). The elements associated with the Wrocław *genius loci* include the stress on vertical accents and monumental flat façades, enlivened by the single sculptural effect of a projecting entrance portico on the southern side (facing the historical town centre). Two towers were originally designed to provide a contrast to this horizontal pull, but only the one on the western side (the Mathematical Tower) was completed. On the other hand, the building's architectural detail seems inspired by the façades of other Jesuit colleges erected earlier in Silesia, with the most direct references to the one in Legnica designed by Knoll. As is typical of Baroque art, the University is a syncretic work, combining architecture with sculpture and painting. This aesthetic unity is particularly striking in the building's staircases and two halls: the Music Hall (destroyed during the last war, currently in the process of reconstruction) and the imperial Leopoldine Hall (*Aula Leopoldina*). With decoration complementing and expanding its architecture rather than merely adorning it, **Aula Leopoldina** is a unique example of the fusion of sculpture, architecture, and painting. On the hall's relatively low ceiling, a plafond painting substitutes an illusion for reality by dissolving the structure and opening it directly into Heaven. Deep niches framing the windows cut off the outside world and give entering light a dramatic quality, simultaneously producing an illusion of some mysterious space hidden behind them. A number of stucco sculptures displayed on projecting cornices enable the viewer to participate in an illusory spectacle of transformation: painted figures from the fresco ceiling attain a more material form as they descend onto the cornices below and become three-dimensional. Here, above the dais, Emperor Leopold – the founder of the University – is represented enthroned in an almost God-like manner. As the eye moves further down, the figures of Leopold's successors, Joseph I and Charles VI, attain the highest degree of reality as sculptures in the round placed symmetrically in front of the columns in the most prominent section of the hall. When one thinks about the splendour of ceremonies that used to take place here, accompanied by heavenly sounds of music coming from a music gallery opposite the dais, adorned with personifications of the Odra and the city of Wrocław, the theatrical aspect of this interior becomes apparent: we face a frozen moment of some spectacle rather than an interior situated at a point in space and time. Viewed from the historical town centre, the University presented itself as a complex of monumental buildings erected on the site previously occupied by the ducal castle. The symbolic replacement of the old fortress by a new stronghold of arts and sciences was underlined by the iconography of allegorical figures installed on the portico. Seen from the north, the University's riverside façade was the most prominent element in the panorama of the city and it soon became one of the most popular Wrocław symbols.

T he people of the Baroque understood the relations among various artistic disciplines and therefore frequently combined different media of artistic expression within a single work of art. Typical of the period was the combination of visual arts and rhetoric, exemplified by the figure of St. John of Nepomuk by St. Maurice's Church – one of three monuments of the martyr saint, who was very popular among Silesian Catholics, erected in Wrocław during the Baroque period. The monument bears an inscription reading 'Come to the defence of a passer-by who greets you with respect'.

A s far as town planning and residential architecture are concerned, there were no axially developed arrangements with sweeping vistas made up of newly-established streets, channels, or gardens, elsewhere so typical of Baroque. To a certain degree, the **palace of Bishop Sintzendorf** was the only exception. Located in today's Zgody Square in the eastern part of the city, the once suburban residence had a garden with flower-beds and hedges symmetrically arranged along the central axis coordinated with the palace's principal façade. Squeezed into narrow Mediaeval plots and subject to regulations forbidding any building to extend outside some preset line, Baroque townhouses were rarely converted into urban palaces. Sometimes they received an added portico entrance with columns (6 Rynek), but most frequently the remodelling was limited to covering façades with painted or stucco decoration in the current Baroque style. Thus, the vertical aspect, to which we referred earlier, combined with a certain flatness and painterly quality apparent in stucco decorations and sculptural ornaments, remained the most characteristic architectural features.

A fter Silesia was taken over by Frederick the Great of Prussia in 1741, Wrocław became Protestant again. During the 1760s, the first Neoclassical buildings were erected in the city, their style reflecting the ideals of the emerging Enlightenment. Concerned with monumentality and the simplification of architectural mass and imbued with a delicate sense of decoration, Neoclassicism was a natural continuation of the specific style of Wrocław architecture. The second **Hatzfeld Palace**, erected after 1766 on the site of the earlier residence in today's Wita Stwosza Street, was designed by Carl Gotthard Langhans the Elder – the greatest Prussian architect of the period, famous for the Brandenburg Gate in Berlin, the architectural symbol of the Prussian state. With its monumental mass accentuated by an imposing rusticated base, the Hatzfeld Palace, of which only the ground floor has survived, was close in spirit to the University complex erected more than twenty years earlier. However, the Hatzfeld Palace lacked any vertical accents: the roof was hidden and there was no tower. The proportions and the quality of architectural detail, in this case entirely Neoclassical, were essential to the building's expression. In some sense, the structure reflected the rationalism of the Protestant Prussian state: its architectural form was not conceived as the glorification of any temporal or religious power but resulted from studies and intellectual analysis. Similar characteristics are apparent in Langhans the Elder's other work in Wrocław, the still extant **Hallenberg-Pachaly Palace** in today's Szajnochy Street (now the University Library) and the lateral wings that he designed for the old Baroque **Spaetgen Palace** in today's Kazimierza Wielkiego Street when it was remodelled into a royal residence (now housing the Archaeological Museum). Designed by Carl Gottfried Geissler as a Neoclassical residence with a portico, the Episcopal Palace on Ostrów Tumski (15 Katedralna Street) belongs to the same architectural school.

I n the early 19th century, so-called 'building regulations' ordering the demolition of wooden houses and replacement of shingle roofs provided a new motivation for building activity in Wrocław. Erected in 1821, the row of houses lining Sukiennice Street (in the middle of the Rynek's central block) was unified by a uniform row of Neoclassical façades and covered with one roof. This early attempt at architectural uniformity in some way preceded many modern housing developments built in Wrocław between the two World Wars; these projects were also characterized by simple and uniform architecture of classical proportions. The most beautiful buildings erected in Wrocław in the early 19th century were designed by Carl Ferdinand Langhans, Carl Gotthard's son and continuator. His most outstanding works include the **Church of Eleven Thousand Virgins** (now the Church of St. Joseph's Care) in today's Jedności Narodowej Street in the northern part of the city; the so called Old Exchange in Solny Square, inspired by the Hatzfeld Palace; the city theatre in Świdnicka Street (later converted into an Opera House and remodelled); and a synagogue in today's Włodkowica Street.

T he single most important event opening new possibilities for urban development in the 19th century was the demolition of the city fortifications, which had been expanded as recently as the late 18th century. Proven useless during the Napoleonic wars, when Wrocław was besieged and conquered by the French army in the winter of 1806–1807, the fortress was decommissioned and given over to the city, which decided to bring down the fortifications in order to plant trees that would form a circle of park promenades (so called **planty**) around the city centre. This green ring has remained one of the most characteristic elements of central Wrocław. The demolition opened the way to connecting the centre of the city with its suburbs: Świdnickie, Oławskie, Mikołajskie, and Odrzańskie. During that period, the city area grew from 163 to 2048 hectares. From the urban planning perspective, this was the beginning of a modern city, with new squares and streets laid outside the Mediaeval chequerboard pattern of the historical centre; a city planned not only for utilitarian reasons but also filled with squares, monuments, and public gardens meant for the eye's pleasure. What was impossible during the Baroque period because of the city walls, could be accomplished once this formidable barrier was gone. Initially, Wrocław developed southwards, along an axis leading from the Rynek along Świdnicka Street to the newly laid-out Tauentzien Square (today's Kościuszki Square), which was situated on the opposite side of the old moat and adorned with the Prussian general's monument. In the southern part of the promenade, the new city **theatre** (later the Opera House) was erected. The opening of the first **railway station** in 1842 south of the historical centre in today's Piłsudskiego Street greatly contributed to the development of the southern part of the city, while today's Traugutta Street became the main artery for its eastern area, where many factories – mostly textile mills – were located. In the 1840s, a second railway station (Dworzec Świebodzki) became a catalyst for building activity in south-western districts.

T he city's territorial expansion allowed developers more freedom, since in the newly-incorporated areas they did not have to deal with narrow parcels of Mediaeval origin. Most of the newcomers to the city settled in new suburbs, where the first **tenement houses** were built for rent. These simple buildings, at the time quite modern, were usually grouped around a rectangular yard. In the late 19th century, six storey structures were not uncommon. Their decoration was usually limited to mass-produced ornaments applied to repetitive, simplified façades.

A modern city consists not only of buildings, but also of parks and gardens. In Wrocław, the country gardens of Prince Hohenlohe in the suburban village of Szczytniki were converted into the city's first public park (the Szczytnicki Park). In the late 19th century two additional big **city parks** (**the South Park and the Osobowice Park**, previously owned by the Korn family) were opened to the public. As early as 1840, the Botanical Garden was established on the Odra sandbank north of Ostrów Tumski and the Zoological Garden was organized in 1864 in the eastern part of the city. Previously dominated by the grey and brick-red tones of its monumental Gothic churches, Wrocław now had the fresh green of plants added to its colours. **Wrocław's green areas**, which have remained essential to the city's beauty, owe their specific character to the mild and relatively humid local climate, which has permitted the cultivation of some exotic species planted in parks and gardens in the late 19th and early 20th centuries, including rhododendrons, azaleas, and plane-trees, quite unique at this latitude. There are also many magnificent oak trees, characteristic of the marshy meadows situated along the Odra. Some parks were enriched with interesting buildings, including a **belvedere** erected in 1867 on the Liebich Hill (today's Partisans' Hill) or the non-extant Victory Column, which used to adorn the promenade in the vicinity of the National Museum.

B eginning in the mid-19th century, the historical revival or so-called 'neo' styles – inspired by Gothic, Renaissance, or Baroque – gain prominence in European architecture. In Wrocław, the city's splendid Gothic tradition provided the ground for an initial adoption of the Neo-Gothic as the leading mode of architectural expression. The central railway station was built in 1857 in the English Gothic Revival style. The new **court and prison** followed the Neo-Gothic form of a feudal castle. Apparently perceived as the most appropriate for public buildings, the Neo-Gothic was also chosen over the Renaissance and Baroque revivals for the **New Exchange** in today's Krupnicza Street, designed by Karl Lüdecke – a student of the Berlin architect Karl Friedrich Schinkel, one of the most outstanding European artists of the period. The New Town Hall, the city's principal administrative building erected in 1863–1865 on the site of the demolished historical Renaissance Linen Drapers' House, was also built in the Gothic Revival style. Historical form was also given to many newly erected industrial buildings and facilities. With its castle-like form and projecting buttresses, the **water tower** in today's Na Grobli Street, built in 1866–1871, resembles a Mediaeval crusaders' keep in the Holy Land. Inside, a steam engine has survived, once the biggest in Europe. Another water tower, built some 30 years later in today's Sudecka Street, is a fantastic castle with Modernist decorations. Red brick, which defined the city's

Gothic form, was also the basic construction and decoration material of many public buildings erected after 1870 with the help of the central government, which, having received large war contributions levied upon France, decided to subsidize several local projects, such as the **Nadodrze railway station**, **the University Library**, **and the complex of clinics** in today's Skłodowskiej-Curie Street. Many Gothic Revival **churches** were also built of brick, including the biggest one, St. Michael's, erected after 1862 in today's Wyszyńskiego Street on the former site of the Ołbin Abbey. Sometimes, in buildings erected in the Renaissance Revival style, brick was used for decorative elements, as was the case for example in the former **building of the Silesian Provincial Government** in today's Powstańców Warszawy Square (currently housing the National Museum).

Despite its territorial expansion beyond the line of old city walls, 19th-century Wrocław was very crowded with buildings. However, even in the most densely populated districts, there were some recreational green areas. Leading around the historical centre, the ring of park promenades established along the still-extant moats was an essential element of the city landscape. There were many new public buildings and several new districts under development: the well-to-do and elegant residential area in the south, with the green oasis of the South Park; the eastern working-class residential and commercial district; the western industrial zone; and the northern area, where the development was less advanced.

The most colourful element of the city-centre buildings were the display windows of elegant shops and restaurants, some of which – like the Piwnica Świdnicka beerhouse located in the Town Hall's cellar – could boast several hundred years' tradition. Forged or cast iron lanterns both illuminated and adorned the streets. Numerous monuments of Prussian monarchs and military commanders (Frederick the Great, Blücher, William I), which decorated the city's principal squares, were also visual manifestations of the state's propaganda. Unfortunately, destroyed during World War II, 19th-century Wrocław is today largely unknown, lost forever. There are some old photographs showing places difficult to identify today, despite captions. The monumental Neo-Renaissance synagogue in today's Łąkowa Street and the edifice of the Silesian Art Museum in Muzealny Square no longer exist. Likewise, the area of today's Grunwaldzki Square, once dominated by the Church of Thanksgiving with a Neo-Gothic spire, would be difficult to recognize for anyone who lived in Wrocław before 1945.

Strolling about Wrocław, one cannot fail to notice its numerous bridges: there are 88 of them in the city. At least two bridges appear as standard features on postcards and photographs. One is **Tumski Bridge** built in 1887. It is impossible to imagine a panorama of Ostrów Tumski without the bridge's characteristic silhouette now, but at the time of its construction, the bridge must have seemed quite shocking as its steel frame acts as a lattice screen closing the principal vista. The other most popular bridge is Wrocław's 'miniature Golden Gate' – the former Imperial Bridge, today known as Grunwaldzki Bridge. Opened in 1910 as the second suspension bridge in Germany, it was the pride of the city and the proof of its self-assured modernity at the threshold of the 20th century.

During the first several years of our century, Wrocław architecture was dominated by a brand of Art Nouveau known as Secession. The best examples of this style are the **department stores**, which were erected in and around the Rynek, frequently on sites freed by the demolition of several historical townhouses. Although the old houses were quite interesting, their loss was sometimes more than compensated for by the elegant architecture of such edifices as the magnificent Barash Brothers store (today's Feniks department store) on the eastern side of the Rynek, built by G. Schneider in 1904. There are also several Art Nouveau department stores lining Rzeźnicza Street. After World War II, they were for many years used as factory space, but recently – following the introduction of a market economy – most of them have been returned to their original function.

Glancing through books on the history of modern architecture, a citizen of Wrocław will come across a familiar structure. It is the **Centennial Hall** (today's People's Hall), at the time the most advanced concrete structure in the world, designed by Max Berg, who was for many years the city architect in Wrocław. While the exterior of the **Covered Market** – the first concrete structure in the city built by R. Plüddemann in 1907 on the former Armoury's site by Piaskowy Bridge – referred to historical forms, the Centennial Hall, erected in 1912–1913, was a futuristic building, free of any historical associations. With the adjacent fair grounds, the Centennial Hall complex is one of only a few examples of the full, uncompromising realization of Berg's architectural ideas. The office towers he designed many years later for the historical city centre have remained on paper. The silhouette of the Centennial Hall's cupola, with its impressive diameter of 67 m., although surrounded by tall trees and invisible from a distance, brings to mind the sacred mountain of Ślęża located 30 kilometres south of the city. Both can be seen only from the upper floors or roofs of the city's taller buildings or from the air, but their presence can somehow be felt in the city. The two 'mounds', one natural and one man-made, remain the main points of reference in the local topographical context. The Centennial Hall's modernity held the spotlight again in 1948, when the World Congress of Intellectuals and a major Silesian exhibition (so-called 'Exhibition of Reclaimed Territories') were organized here. In 1948, only one element was added to Berg's original plan: an almost 100-metre-tall spire, designed by Stanisław Hempel, was placed on the axis leading to the Centennial Hall's main entrance.

Designing the fair ground facilities around the Centennial Hall, Berg worked closely with another famous European architect, Hans Poelzig, who was also responsible for many outstanding structures erected in Wrocław in the International-Modern style, including an office building in today's Ofiar Oświęcimskich Street. Another building frequently featured in studies on 20th-century architecture is the **department store** designed by the famous Expressionist architect Erich Mendelsohn, built in 1927 in today's Szewska Street. Somewhat reminiscent of the navigating bridge of a grand pre-war ocean liner, the building seems to sail majestically towards St. Mary Magdalene's Church. Even today, it remains the most modern and beautiful of all department store buildings in Wrocław. Another great store, erected several years later in today's Kościuszki Square, although still the biggest and most popular of the city's retail establishments, was no match for Mendelsohn's work.

By the 1920s, the town centre and inner districts were so densely populated that it became necessary to build new suburbs on the outskirts of the city. In 1924, new plans for urban development were approved and then carried out until the outbreak of World War II. The plans called for a tripling of the area within city limits, which was accomplished by 1928 by extending Wrocław stretched to the west, south and east. The new developments included Popowice and several suburbs which are very popular residential areas today: Grabiszynek in the south, and Sępolno and Biskupin in the eastern part of the city. Organized in 1929 on the grounds of Szczytnicki Park, an important **international architectural exhibition** – 'Home and Work Place' (WUWA) – left many forward-looking structures designed by the period's best architects in the neighbourhood of Zielonego Dębu Street. In the nearby Sępolno, a modern housing project was completed. Its uniform but attractive architecture, interesting layout combined with a self-sufficient programme comprising green areas, shops, schools, sport facilities and public buildings, made it a model residential development. If it were not for the increased road traffic, impossible to predict in 1932, Sępolno would have remained an ideal residential area, with the adjacent park and sport facilities built for the 1936 Olympic Games in Berlin adding to its attraction.

The most tragic period in Wrocław's history – its three-month ordeal as the besieged *Festung Breslau* – came to an end on 6 May 1945. Its results were dramatic: with an average destruction rate of 68%, the southern area suffered 90% damage and half of the historical centre was in ruins. Many architectural monuments were badly affected. For example, the Cathedral suffered 75% damage and the cost of its reconstruction topped $3,000,000 in 1970 prices. Unfortunately, not all historical buildings could be saved. However, the original layout of the historical centre has been preserved, with most of the architectural monuments repaired or reconstructed. Frequently, construction work provided an opportunity for archaeological and architectural studies, and many monuments were restored to their original form stripped of later additions. Today, as we write, work on certain elements of architectural detail is still in progress, for example the construction of spires on the Cathedral's two towers. As yet, some historical buildings (townhouses in Ruska Street, part of the old Arsenal) have not found new users, many are still in the process of reconstruction (St. Elizabeth's Church). Certain parts of the city, too badly damaged to be rebuilt, have been filled with new architecture with only occasional references to the historical form. Sometimes original architectural detail from damaged structures was built into reconstructed townhouses. In several cases, surviving fragments were left on the site, like the remnants of the Hatzfeld Palace which were incorporated into the new modern structure. There are also several areas relatively close to Wrocław's historical centre, which were levelled during the war and still remain undeveloped. There are plans for the redevelopment of Dominikański Square and for a new commercial centre to be built in Powstańców Śląskich Street, a major communication artery that extends the city's principal urban axis leading south from the Rynek along Świdnicka Street. Another priority is the construction of several multi-storey garages, including those to be situated between Kazimierza Wielkiego and Ofiar Oświęcimskich Streets and on an empty lot between Św. Katarzyny and Krowia Streets. The fact that many attractive centrally located lots have remained undeveloped so long time after the war gives Wrocław a special opportunity, contributing to its unique character among Polish cities. Modernist residential developments, constructed of prefabricated elements, were built mostly on the outskirts of the city, and small empty lots were left alone. Only in the late 1980s did they begin to draw investors, attracted by their central location and the economic aspect of having all the necessary infrastructure already in place. The new projects, fondly referred to as 'fillings' (as they fill in the gaps between existing buildings), have become a local speciality and something of a mass movement. Usually, their architecture refers to the form of adjacent 19th century townhouses, but sometimes fantasy, for so long suppressed by the 'concrete slab' mentality, reigns supreme. It is somewhat symbolic that it is only now (1993) that the replica of the Renaissance Golden Dog House is being completed on its original site, which was the last empty lot remaining in Wrocław's Rynek as a result of the Second World War.

MAJOR DATES IN THE HISTORY OF THE CITY

935-972 — 'Vratsao', probably the city's first name, appears on coins minted by the Bohemian king Boleslaus

1000 — a diocese of the Gniezno Archbishopric is established in Wrocław

1112 — the first church on the left bank of the Odra River, the small St. Adalbert's Church, is presumably founded

1149 — the first mention of a castle chapel on Ostrów Tumski (Cathedral Island)

1st half of the 12th c. — a Benedictine Abbey, founded by the magnate Piotr Włost, is established at Ołbin (St. Michael's Church, donated to the Abbey, is mentioned in 1139)

1158 — the construction of a new cathedral by Bishop Walter of Malonne, replacing an earlier one, is mentioned for the first time

1175 — the first mention of a rich Wrocław house (the magnate Mikora's *curia* at Ołbin)

1218 — St. Egidius', the oldest church to survive to this day, is founded

1224 — friars of the urban Dominican order are brought to the city

1226 — St. Mary Magdalene's Church is presumably founded

1241 — the first mention of a merchant house in Wrocław

1241 — Wrocław obtains its first municipal charter based on Magdeburg Laws (*Ius Teutonicum*); soon afterwards the still-existing layout of the Rynek (Town Square) and the streets in the historical town centre is established

1243-1248 — St. Elizabeth's parish church is founded

1257 — Franciscan monks and Clarist nuns - orders typical of medieval urban communities - settle on the site currently occupied by the Ursuline convent in today's Nankiera Square

1261 — the renewed grant of Magdeburg statutes to the city

1263 — Nowe Miasto (New Town) is founded east of the Nowy Targ (New Market Square); it was a separate entity only until 1327

1266 — the first mention of merchant stalls in Wrocław

1272 — the earliest recorded instruction for Wrocław burghers recommending that houses be built of stone or brick

1288 — in an act of reconciliation with the bishop, Duke Henry Probus founds the collegiate Church of the Holy Cross

2nd half of the 13th c. - early 14th c. — the building of an outer wall with 50 towers; the city limits are extended to the line of today's Podwale Street

1343 — there are 11 flour mills in Wrocław

1351 — Emperor Charles IV founds St. Dorothy's Church in what is now Świdnicka Street

14th c. — most of Wrocław's Gothic churches are expanded, obtaining their present form

1387 — the beginnings of municipal water supply

1403 — there are 304 inns in the city

1st half of the 15th c. — new gates and approaches are built

1452-1458 — the erection of the tower of St. Elizabeth's Church, the tallest in Wrocław

1463 — the Bernardines, brought to Wrocław in response to the Hussite heresy, build a brick church

1479 — the first bastille, a defensive structure adapted to the use of newly-introduced firearms, is erected at St. Nicholas' Gate

1493 — a wood engraving showing the earliest known view of Wrocław is published in Hartmann Schedel's *Liber Chronicarum*

c. 1500 — the Town Hall obtains its present late Gothic form

1512 — Magister Bartholomeus Stein gives the first extensive description of the city

1517 — the Cathedral obtains its first uniformly Renaissance portal

1521-1528 — the Golden Crown House, the first Renaissance residence in Wrocław, is built at the corner of the Rynek and Oławska Street

1526-1531 — a magnificent Renaissance house, still partially preserved, is built for the patrician Heinrich Rybisch in today's Ofiar Oświęcimskich Street

1526 — the city fortifications are reinforced for fear of Turkish invasion

1587-1529 — the Griffons House is erected in the Rynek by the Dutch architect Frederick Gross in the Dutch Renaissance style

1634 — the idea of building up-to-date fortifications around the city takes shape during the Thirty Years' War

1638 — the first Jesuits, the most ardent promoters of the baroque, settle in Wrocław

1666 — the first baroque chapel is built at the Church of the Blessed Virgin Mary on Sand Island

1679-1682 — the baroque St. Elizabeth's Chapel is erected adjacent to the Cathedral's chancel

1685-1692 — the baroque St. Anthony's Church is built

1689-1698 — the Jesuit Church of the Blessed Name of Jesus is built

1716-1724 — the baroque Elector's Chapel is built north-east of the Cathedral's chancel according to the design of the famous Viennese architect Fischer von Erlach

1722-1728 — the Jesuit Church obtains magnificent baroque décor

1728 — construction work begins on the University founded in 1702

1765-1775 — designed by Carl Gotthard Langhans, the new Hatzfeld Palace in today's Wita Stwosza Street becomes the first neoclassical residence in Wrocław

1807 — the city obtains grounds previously occupied by fortifications: the demolition of the walls opens the way for connecting the city centre and suburbs into a unified urban system

1822-1824 — the Old Exchange edifice is built in Solny Square

1825 — a steam engine begins pumping water to the water supply system

1837-1841 — a city theatre (later an opera house) is built in Świdnicka Street

1842 — the first railway line is opened linking Wrocław with Oława

1847 — the first municipal gasworks is put into operation

1856 — a steamboat connection opens between Wrocław and Szczecin

1856 — a new neo-Gothic railway station is opened

1856 — a railway car and engine factory is established (now known as Pafawag)

1883-1886 — the neo-Renaissance building of the Silesian Provincial Government is built (now houses the National Museum)

1885 — the city has 236 factories, most of them established during the 1870s

1891 — a power station is put into operation

1910 — the suspension Imperial Bridge (now Grunwaldzki Bridge) is opened

1913 — the construction of the Centennial Hall (now the People's Hall) with a reinforced concrete dome, then the largest in the world, is completed

1925-1930 — the development of the satellite residential suburbs of Popowice, Sępolno, Biskupin, Pilczyce, Muchobór, and Grabiszynek

1927 — Erich Mendelsohn, one of the best-known expressionist architects, builds a department store in Szewska Street

1928 — the administrative area of the city triples, mainly as a result of westward expansion

1929 — a large architectural exhibition (WUWA) opens in Wrocław with several interesting buildings erected specially for the occasion in the Park Szczytnicki area

1936 — an East-West motorway is opened south of the city

1945 — the city is turned into a closed stronghold and suffers severe damage as a result of heavy fighting

1954-1958 — the area of today's Kościuszki Square is redeveloped as the only example of Socialist Realism architecture in Wrocław

1960 — the first stage of the reconstruction programme is completed; the concrete slab technology based on prefabricated elements is introduced in the construction of several large housing developments (Huby, Gajowice, Popowice, Nowy Dwór, Kozanów, Gaj, Różanka)

1970 — a rotunda designed to house the panoramic painting of the Battle of Racławice, originally displayed in Lwów (Lviv), is completed; it opens to the public in 1985

1970-1991 — the construction of an inner ring road around the historical city centre

1973 — the city area is significantly enlarged as a result of the incorporation of neighbouring villages

1993 — the city's first international air connection links Wrocław and Frankfurt

1995-1997 — general repairs of the Rynek and Solny Square in preparation for the Eucharistic Congress

1. St. John the Baptist's Cathedral. View from the west.

↑ 2. Ostrów Tumski (Cathedral Island) seen across the Odra River.

3. St. John the Baptist's Cathedral. East side, left to right: St. Elizabeth's Chapel (1680–1700), St. Mary's Chapel (1354–1365), and the Elector's Chapel (1716–1724).

4. St. John the Baptist's Cathedral. Chancel, the oldest part of
the church (13th c.). In front — the 1727 figures of SS Jerome
and Gregory executed by J.G. Unbański.

5. Cathedral. Altar in St. Elizabeth's Chapel (G. Scianzi, E. Ferrata,
1679–1682).

6. Cathedral. Detail of the Renaissance tombstone of J. Turzon –
   the bishop of Wrocław and an outstanding humanist (1537).

→7. Cathedral. Renaissance portal of the sacristy with a relief representing the martyrdom of St. John the Baptist (1517).

8. Ostrów Tumski (Cathedral Island). St. Egidius' – the oldest extant church in Wrocław (1213–1218 and 15th c.), with a Romanesque arcade frieze preserved on the apse wall.

9. Church of the Holy Cross seen from the Botanical Garden: the two – storey. Gothic hall church was founded in 1288 by Duke Henry IV Probus.

↑ 10. Archdiocesan Museum, Kanonia Street. Exhibition of Gothic art.

→11. Interior of the Archdiocesan Museum.

↑ 12. Ostrów Tumski (Cathedral Island). View of St. Martin's Chapel (13th – 15th century). In the background, the imposing form of the Church of the Holy Cross.

13. Baroque statue of St. John of Nepomuk in front of the Church of the Holy Cross (K. Tausch, J. J. Urbański, 1730–1732). In the background: *Orphanotrophaeum*, an orphanage for noblemen's children.

↑ 14. Gothic Church of the Blessed Virgin Mary on the Sand Island (ca. 1334 – 1380), formerly Augustinian, erected on the site of an earlier Romanesque structure.

15. Church of the Blessed Virgin Mary. Hall interior with a nave and two aisles.

16.   Church of the Blessed Virgin Mary. Vaulting of the northern aisle.

↑ 17.   The Baroque building of the former Augustinian abbey on Sand Island, 1709–1715, adjoining the Church of the Blessed Virgin Mary. Now houses a branch of the University Library.

18.   Interior of the former Augustinian Sisters' St. Anne's Church in Św. Jadwigi Street (1687–1691). Now the Orthodox Church of St. Cyril, St. Methodius, and St. Anne.

↑ 19. A bird's eye view of left-bank Wrocław, with several Baroque
monasteries: the Premonstratensian monastery with the Gothic
St. Vincent's Church, the Ursuline (formerly Clarist) convent,
and the monastery of the Red Star Knights of the Cross.

20. Former monastery of the Red Star Knights of the Cross in
Szewska Street (now housing the University Library). Former
prelacy hall with the dome of the belvedere (ca. 1715).

21. Former monastery of the Red Star Knights of the Cross, designed by J. B. Mathieu (1676–1715). Overlooking Grodzka Street, the elegant Baroque façade of the northern wing with the belvedere.

22. Baroque Jesuit Church of the Blessed Name of Jesus (1689–1698) erected on the site formerly occupied by a part of the demolished ducal castle. South-western gable wall.

23.   Interior of the Church of the Blessed Name of Jesus (K. Tausch,
      J. W. Siegwitz, F. J. Mangoldt, 1722–1733). Illusionistic fres-
      coes by J. M. Rottmayer (1703–1706).

← 24. University. The Matematyczna (mathematical) Tower viewed from the south.

← 25. University. Former Jesuit college founded in 1702. The Baroque structure was erected on the site of an earlier castle (1728–1741). Northern façade.

↑ 26. University. Interior of the Leopoldine Hall, erected in 1730––1732 in honour of Emperor Leopold I, the founder of the Jesuit college.

→ 27. University. Leopoldine Hall. Bust of J. A. Schaffgotsch on the music gallery (F. J. Mangoldt, ca. 1731).

←28. Baroque Chapel of Count Hochberg (C. Hackner, 1723–27), adjoining the Gothic St. Vincent's Church in Nankiera Square.

↑ 29. Tomb of Duke Henry VI (after 1335), the last of the Wrocław dukes, in the mausoleum of the Silesian Piasts in the present-day Ursuline St. Clare's Church in Nankiera Square.

→30. Tombstone of Anne, daughter of Duke Henry V, in the mausoleum of the Silesian Piasts in the Ursuline St. Clare's Church in Nankiera Square.

←31. A bird's eye view of the Old Town with the Rynek (Town Square).

←32 The Rynek (Town Square). New Town Hall (A. Stüler, 1860–1863), built on the site of the demolished Gothic Linen Drapers' House. In the background: western façade of the Gothic Town Hall (15th c.).

↑ 33. Town Hall, now housing the Historical Museum. Eastern façade with a 14th c. chapel oriel, a magnificent Gothic gable dating from the turn of the 15th and 16th c., and an astronomical clock from 1569.

→34. Town Hall. Council Hall (15th c.). On the left, a Renaissance portal dating from 1528.

←35. Town Hall. Oriel window in the southern façade (1480s), richly decorated with stone sculptures and reliefs. Below: entrance to the Piwnica Świdnicka cellar.

↑ 36. Town Hall. Elegant interior of the first floor Grand Hall with a portal dating from about 1485.

→37. Town Hall. Ducal Hall (previously St. Dorothy's chapel). The Gothic vaulting is supported by a massive pillar. In the background: portals leading to Senior Councillor's Hall and the Grand Hall.

↑ 38. The Rynek (Town Square), western side: a view from the Town Hall tower. On the right, in the background: the Gothic St. Elizabeth's Church, one of Wrocław's two Medieval parish churches (14th–16th c.).

39. A view from the Town Hall tower towards the north-ea the inner block and the north-east corner of the Rynek (To Square).

↑ 40. Eastern side of the Rynek (Town Square). On the left: former Barash Brothers store (G. Schneider, 1905), the most beautiful of Worcław's Art Nouveau department stores (now the Feniks department store).

41. Solny Square (Salt Square) situated next to the Rynek (Town Square), laid out after 1241 along with the Rynek and the gridiron street pattern of the historical centre

←42. A southern view of the Gothic St. Mary Magdalene's Church in Szewska Street (14th–15th c.), one of the two principal parish churches of Medieval Wrocław, today the parish church of the Polish Catholic National Church.

↓ 43 St. Mary Magdalene's Church. Romanesque portal (late 12th c.), transferred from the Benedictine abbey at Ołbin following its demolition in 1529.

44.   St. Mary Magdalene's Church. Renaissance pulpit by F. Gross
(1579–1581).

45. The Dominican St. Adalbert's Church in Św. Katarzyny Street.
The extant Gothic structure (ca. 1251–1270, 1300–1330)
was erected on the site of a parish church founded in 1112.

46. St. Adalbert's Church. Interior of the Chapel of Blessed Czesław
     Odrowąż (B. Miller, 1711–1724). Impressive Baroque sculp-
     tures by L. Weber. In the middle, the alabaster sarcophagus
     of Blessed Czesław.

47.　The former Bernardine church and monastery complex (15th–16th c.) in Bernardyńska Street, now housing the Museum of Architecture. Southern view.

←48.　The Romanesque Room at the Museum of Architecture with a display of architectural fragments. On the right: the 'Jaksa Tympanum' from the Ołbin Abbey.

↑ 49.　Church of St. Stanislaus, St. Venceslas, and St. Dorothy (2nd half of the 14th c.) in Świdnicka Street. Sculptures of the Rococo tomb of Baron G. Spaetgen (F. J. Mangoldt, 1752–1753).

→50.　Church of St. Slanislaus, St. Venceslas, and St. Dorothy. The 18th c. Baroque décor inside the Gothic hall church. In the foreground: a statue of St. John the Baptist (L. Weber, ca. 1710).

↑ 51. Interior of the Church of Divine Providence (1747–1750) in Kazimierza Wielkiego Street. Late Baroque structure with oval galleries fitted into a rectangular interior. Today, a Lutheran church.

52. Church of the Eleven Thousand Virgins, now St. Joseph's (C. F. Langhans, 1820–1823) in Jedności Narodowej Street. Gothic sculptures built into the façade were transferred from St. Nicholas' gate, demolished in 1820.

↑ 53. The so-called New Exchange (K. Lüdecke, 1865–1867) in Krupnicza Street (now housing the Gwardia Sports Club). A Neo-Gothic edifice with rich figural decoration.

54. The Central Railway Station in Piłsudskiego Street. One of the earliest train stations in Wrocław, it was built in the English Gothic Revival style (W. Grapow, 1855–1857; expanded 1899–1904).

↑ 55. Świdnicka Street. Left to right: the Opera House and the Monopol Hotel, with the Church of St. Stanislaus, St. Venceslas, and St. Dorothy in the background.

56. The Opera House, formerly the city theatre (C. F. Langhans, 1837–1841). Rebuilt twice following fires, the building's present form is significantly different from the original design.

57. The Opera House. The remodelled interior (K. Schmidt, 1871–1872).

58. The court and prison building in Podwale Street has the
    form of a romantic castle in the Gothic Revival style
    (K. F. Busse, 1845).

↑ 59. Colonnade on Partisans' Hill, formerly known as Liebich Hill (K. Schmidt, 1866–1867). The Neo-Renaissance park was established on the site previously occupied by the so-called Sash Bastion.

→60. Municipal Baths in Teatralna Street (W. Werdelmann, 1895–1897, 1907–1909). Built in a historical revival style, the structure nevertheless incorporates some contemporaneous Art Nouveau detail.

61. St. Michael's Church in Nowowiejska Street, built in the Gothic
    Revival style on the site of the former Benedictine abbey at
    Ołbin (A. Langer, 1862–1871).

62. The National Museum in Powstańców Warszawy Square. The building was originally the seat of the Silesian Provincial Government (K. F. Endell, 1883–1886). Its architecture is reminiscent of the Dutch Renaissance and Baroque.

63. The former School of Arts and Crafts in Prusa Street, now the Faculty of Architecture of Wrocław Technical University. A picturesque combination of Neo-Romanesque and Art Nouveau forms (K. Klimm, 1901–1903).

↑ 64. St. Charles Boromeo's Church in Krucza Street. A monumental Neo-Romanesque structure, whose form was inspired by German Romanesque cathedrals (J. Maas, 1911–1913).

←65. Water tower with an observation deck in Sudecka Street. Free interpretation of historical styles in the expressive form of a fantastic castle (K. Klimm, 1903–1904).

→66. Jewish Cemetery in Ślężna Street. Tomb of F. Lassalle (1825–1864), a socialist activist and the founder of the first workers' party in Germany.

↓ 67. Jewish Cemetery in Ślężna Street. Sepulchres and tombstones dating from the 19th and 20th c. Now a branch of the Historical Museum.

↑ 68. Covered Market in Piaskowa Street. An innovative structure supported by parabolic arches of reinforced concrete disguised by a historical façade (R. Plüddemann, H. Küster, 1906–1908).

69. Oławski Bridge (formerly Maurice Bridge) linking Wróblewskiego Square with Na Grobli Street. The three-span stone bridge is a charming combination of architecture and sculptural decoration (1883).

↑ 70. Zwierzyniecki Bridge (formerly Passbrücke). A single-span steel construction on stone supports, decorated with Classical Revival detail (Frühwirth, K. Klimm, 1895–1897).

71. Grunwaldzki Bridge (formerly Imperial Bridge), the most popular of Wrocław bridges. Its steel construction is suspended on two massive granite pylons (R. Weyrauch, M. Mayer, R. Plüddemann, 1908–1910).

↑ 72. The former grounds of the 1913 Centennial Exhibition commemorating the 100th anniversary of the Battle of Leipzig. View from the west: the dominating Centennial Hall (today People's Hall) by M. Berg; the Pergola and the Four Domes Pavilion by H. Poelzig.

73. Centennial Hall (now People's Hall). This Modernist structure of reinforced concrete remains impressive even today (M. Berg, 1911–1913). In front of the main entrance, the 'Iglica' spire (S. Hempel), erected in 1948 as the emblem of the Exhibition of the Reclaimed Territories.

↑ 74. Pergola (H. Poelzig, 1913). A colonnade surrounding a pond with a fountain, situated north of the Centennial Hall, erected as a part of the Centennial Exhibition complex.

75. The Japanese garden in the Szczytnicki Park, the oldest and largest in the city.

76. Department store in Szewska Street. Built of steel, travertine, bronze, and glass, this Expressionist work still remains modern and beautiful (E. Mendelsohn, 1927).

↑ 77. A house with flats for single people (now a hotel) in Kopernika Street (H. Sharoun, 1929) was one of the buildings erected for the WUWA ('Home and Work Place') architectural exhibition of 1929.

78. Sępolno. A model housing development, built after 1928 in the eastern part of the city (P. Heim, H. Wahlich).

↑ 79. Post-Modernist St. Mary's Church in Wejherowska Street, whose construction started in 1982, demonstrates the architects` fascination with geometrical transformations (W. Jarząbek, H. Hryniewicz, J. Matkowski).

80. Pomorski Bank Kredytowy in Malarska Street (M. Molicka, E. Zlat, A. Adamek), cleverly fitted between historical houses. The design won the 1992 edition of the local architectural competition for buildings filling in the gaps between surviving historical structures.